Way to home

--A.Sankareswari . M.E.

For the Souls blessed by Lord

To

find path to home.

Contents

Sl.No	Chapter	Page No
	Preface	4
1	World knowledge	6
2	Properties of world	10
3	Characteristics of qualities	15
4	God's Worlds	17
5	Our Home.(Veedu)	20
6	Three Real Objects	22
7	Most degraded state of the soul	26
8	Sivam – Shakthi	28
9	Merciful Punishment	31
10	saiva siddhanta philosophy	34
11	The Five Works of God	53
12	Gods levels	57
13	Methods of Worship	64
14	Desire To reach home	68
15	Thirukkural - The Way to Reach Home	74
16	Yogic effort-Way to home.	90
17	Get home	96
18	The mystery of the creation of the world	100

Preface

There are many philosophies in the world – each religion has developed its own philosophies, saiva siddhanta philosophy is one of the oldest philosophies that originated in Tamil Nadu (India) about 3000 years ago.

They explain the purpose and formation of the earth. The nature, ultimate freedom of the soul and the ultimate happiness of the soul.

Philosophy cannot be read and understood in its entirety, and what we see now is the fundamentals of philosophy.

Mature souls learn philosophy by its own experience, and the ordinary soul reads and learns philosophy.

For example, do you know swimming, if you know, what do you know? Swimming is an act of floating and moving in the water, which is done using the hands and feet. You know what to swim, if you know this much only , but if you really know swimming means you have to swim in the water,

Another example - do you know the Tamil language? Yes, Tamil language is the oldest language in the world and is a Dravidian language spoken in India , Sri Lanka, Singapore and many other countries. If you know so much, you know what is Tamil, but if you don't know how to speak and write that language, it means you don't know Tamil.

In that sense, in this book we are going to study the fundamentals of saiva siddhanta philosophy.About formation of earth, and purpose of our life in earth , ways to find home.

Without God's wish we cannot reach the home, selected souls only have desire to reach home. God know when to give desire of home to all souls .

By God Grace , through this book your soul will get attracted to learn more about Veedu (home) through saiva siddhanta philosophy .

-A.Sankareswari

World knowledge .

The Saiva theorists delved deeper into the search for God and formulated what they found into philosophies. By examining how and why this world was created, they discovered many truths.

All we know that this world is made up of five elements, namely Space, Air, Fire, water, and soil. And all human beings are interacting with these elements , with our five sense organs they are ears, skin, eyes, tongue and nose. Without these five organs we cannot interact with the world and we cannot understand the presence of the world.

This world is made up of many things, which are inanimate objects, and living beings.

Living Organisms are divided according to the knowledge it possesses , and the knowledge is through the sense organs .

Examples:
single sense - tree , plants , grass
Two sense - snail and shells - touch and Taste
three senses - Ant , millipedes - touch , taste , smell
four sense – fliers, touch , taste , smell , vision
five sense - Animals , touch , taste , smell , vision , hear.
six sense - human , touch , taste , smell , vision , hear , inferring with analytics

Humans are the only living being in this world , that we know for six sense.

The six kind of knowledge we have are through our six sense organs, Knowledge through sight , knowledge of taste , Knowledge through touching, knowledge through smelling, knowledge through hearing . and the sixth sense is mind knowledge .

Every incident happens to us give some feelings , Mind is a knowledge tool which is used to understand and registered all the pleasure and unpleasure from the incident, The knowledge of suffering and anger is through knowledge of the mind.

Except mind all other organ we can see , we do not know where the mind organ is located , some believe that mind is not an organ but some believe the mind also has an organ, but it is not visible to our eyes. It is in a subtle form. Some say it's located very close to the heart.

So only we feel happiness and sad near to our heart, sudden undesirable news will give pain near the heart. It's clearly indicating that mind is an organ responsible for understand the happy and sad, and it is location is present near our heart.

Other than human , for all other living beings, emotions related to any incident will be vanished once the incident is completed. For human alone emotions will be memorized by mind , after some time we may forgot the incident itself, by emotions created by incident will be recorded in mind.

Example: you might have scolded someone one year back , if you recollect the incident , you may remember the anger shown on him only , but reason for the anger you might have forgotten .

Not only humans but some animals also have a mind. but That mind will not be in fully matured condition as for human beings, it will work partially. but it will work fully only for human beings only . Animals with partial working mind are eligible to be reared as domestic animals.

For human beings also , the mind is not fully functioning at birth. It's only partially functional. As it grows, it matures.

Human being is superior in the knowledge with their six-sense organ .

Some animals ,birds are predicting tsunami, earth quake . But human unable predicting . then how to say human being are superior in knowledge ?

Animals are living according to nature , they mingled with nature , example they take the food grown naturally they never do cultivation according to their food habit , animals not evolved , life style of animal is same form day the exists , human being are evolved over year , although we and 1000 year back human are same, our life style , habits, attitude all changed . Due to evolution slowly we moved away from the nature , and living in a protected atmosphere in hot weather we use AC, in winter we use woolen coat .

We became cultured living being after following cultivation of crops.

Although we unable to sense the nature by our own intent, we human are more intelligent than any animals in this earth .

Hence the presence of this world is in our sense only , earth knowledge is based on our sense only.

Know living being in the earth, who have more knowledge of the earth is human only.

****

Properties of world

The world is filled with living things and non-living things. All objects have some properties. For example, in a jasmine flower, it has certain qualities such as white color, softness and aroma . Thus, all objects have some qualities. There are a number of products in this world. So, there are many qualities.

The Saiva theorists says , objects are not having properties . properties joined together and framed the object. Ex: white color , softness, aroma etc. are the properties joined together and jasmine flower is visible to us.

They started analyzing all the possible properties in the world , and that each object has many properties , they found number properties are more than the number of objects in the world , they started to classify the properties and classified all the properties under three .

They are

1. Sattvika guna,
2. Rajasa guna, and
3. Tamasa Gunam

The term Guna has the meanings of character, character and nature.

The three qualities that arise from nature are:

- Sattvam (goodness/creativity/harmony),

- Rajas (activeness/pulse/confusion),

-Tamas (ignorance/immorality/destructiveness)

Everything in world can be classified based on these three characteristics.

Even color also , all we know the basic of colors , RBY, that is red blue and yellow combination of these three colors will give all other colors. yellow is sattva, red is Rajas and blue is tamas. Similarly, combination of this properties is present in object.

Our weekdays start from Sunday to Saturday , each day have the three qualities , Sunday means sun's day , bright day , creativity will be more on Sunday, which have more of sattvam gunam . Monday is moon's day , combination presence of sattva and rajas gunam. Tuesday is day of venues , angry will be more on the day , which more it has more rajas gunam . Wednesday will have all the gunam in equal proportion , hence Wednesday is called as best in any week. Tamil proverb says "although you got gold, getting Wednesday is rare" . Thursday tamas gunam also started , sattva will be less. Friday tamas gunam will come which leads to kamam , Saturday tamas will be more compare other two gunams leads to tired or rest.

Since Tuesday rajas will be more , possible of angry will be more and on Friday tamas started sexual feeling will be more, although Saturday tamas will be more but it leads to tired . to control angry and sexual feeling , peoples use to go to temple on the day for mind change.

A day also classified based on this gunams , early morning is sattva , mid-day is raja and night is tamas . for learning morning is the best time because of sattva gunam , and for doing work day time is good, and for taking rest night is good.

Early morning up to 8 am if you see sun and close your eyes it will be yellow in color , in mid-day around 11am if you see and close your eyes it will be red in color , evening after 4pm if you see and close your eyes blue color will be visible. Color may vary based on the day , month and our mind also .

Changeover of gunam is difficult to handle, if one fellow talking to you politely suddenly started shouting means his gunam is changed from sattva to rajas , hence in our culture during the change over time they do poojas and prayer known sandhyavandanam , means killing the mixing period of gunam.

A year also divided in similarly way , January month is starting of a year , in Tamil culture also Thai month falls on January month. In this month sattva gunam will be stared and it will be more , after 3 months i.e., in April month Rajas will be more , in yearend November and December tamas will be more.

Normally in Tamil culture during July , august month newly married couples will be separated , because rajas will be in peak at the time , leads to angry and mis-understanding between newly united pairs .

Human life also can be classified based on three gunam, starting of life is learning period sattva will be more , middle of life is working and earning period rajas will be more , end part of life tamas gunam will be more leads to tired and rest .

Food also classified based on this three gunam, in fact food is the main reason for formation of this Gunam inside ourself, if you take food which is of sattva gunam your studies , creativity will increase . if you take food with rajas gunam your Woking skill will increase , soldiers will take this rajas food , mainly red meat . if you take tamas food will increase your sexual feeling , lead you to tired , sleep.

How to identify the food gunam is by the color of food , yellow or white shade food , ex. Milk , curd are good for sattva gunam. Red shade color food ex; meat , are good for rajas, blue color or black color food are for tamas gunam.

By taste also gunam is classified , sweet is sattva, spicy chill is rajas, sour is for tamas.

Sattva gunam is represented as yellow/white, Rajas gunam in red and Tamas gunam as blue/black. White represents purity, red represents performance, and black represents ignorance.

A white garment represents a pure state of being free from dirt. The red blood flowing through the body always runs and indicates activity. In the dark we cannot see anything, and darkness means black. Therefore, black was used as a parable to denote tamas gunam.

****

Characteristics of qualities

Sattva – balance, harmony, goodness, purity, divinity, creativity, creativity, truth, lovingness, controlling desire, doing good deeds, doing sweets, assertiveness, peace, honesty, virtue, impassableness

Rajas – action, efficiency, activity, performance (whether the action is good or bad) , selfishness, pride, dissension, constant acting

Tamas – imbalance, disorganization, restlessness, improper habits, unruly nature, chaos, impurity, destructive nature, fainting, discouragement, negative thoughts, depression, Inactivity, insensitivity, laziness, fatigue, cruelty, stupidity, aggression, violence, intentional act of hurting others, doing bad.

The color of the sattvik gunam is yellow/white , its God Brahma, the wife of Brahma is Saraswati, the color of Saraswati's dress and the color of the lotus in which they sit is the god of white knowledge. That is why we consider Brahma to be the God of righteousness.

The royal character is red with its god Vishnu and his wife Lakshmi, which is why Lakshmi sits with a red lotus. Lakshmi is offered as the goddess of wealth and therefore we pray for Vishnu and Lakshmi as the gods of material wealth.

Tamasa's quality is blue/black in its color and lord Shiva and his wife fire power. That's why we pray to Lord Shiva as the god of the destructive delusion of pleasure.

Not only nonliving being , all living being characters also classified in to this three.

All this gunam won’t be alone , it will be different proposition of combination. No one object is full of one gunam , means 100% or 0% of a gunam is not possible .

All objects are classified in to in this three gunam ,and all this three gunam will be will present in all object .

****

Divinely Worlds:

we know that living being are classified based on their knowledge , and knowledges are through senses, and we human are superior in knowledge because of six senses .

And plants are having only one sense, is there anything below one sense ? below one is zero senses. Between 1 and zero there are decimals . some living being are below 1 sense and they are just above 0, examples some stone , minerals are having senses but it will not be 1 , it may be 0.001 sense. And they also getting little knowledge of the world through there limited senses.

Is there anything above six senses, yes beyond our six senses , there also some living beings beyond six senses , they have more knowledge then human. They also living in this world , since we have only six senses , we cannot feel the presence of more than six senses , those who living with more than six sense are called as divinely persons like God.

Many Gods are there in every culture , in Tamil Culture we know many gods Lord Ganesha, Lord Muruga, Lord Karrupu Swamy, Lord Maha Muni, Lord Ayyanar, Lord Marriyamma , and keep on going .

All this God is living in this world , and they living in different dimension , to see them we required more knowledge , we required more than six senses.

Depends on our knowledge only world will appear to us , although they living in this world , for them this world looks different. And good are not having same amount of knowledge , it will vary between them ,based upon their Knowle world will appears to them . So that stage of world is known as Gods World .

Divinely worlds are a world beyond our six senses. We need more than six senses to understand it. When our knowledge matures and transcends knowledge and reaches the levels above it, we can feel the world in which Gods lives.

In this world, there is a limit to all pleasure & tragedies. We can't feel any pleasure and sorrow for a long time. For example, if it's a pleasure for a person to get drenched in the rain, he can't accept it happily for a long time. likewise, you can't feel the pain for a long time. We can only accept it up to a certain level, we cannot feel pleasure and suffering beyond a limit.

There's a time for everything. Pleasure only for a period of time, time limit is there for the suffering as well. If that time is over, the events of pleasure and sorrow will disappear.

In divinely world also there is a limit for all , and Gods worlds also not permanent .

Divinely world , may be available in this world itself , or in some other planets. it not visible to us .

But There is link between our world and divinely Gods world , divinely persons are capable to give blessing to us , with their graces , good and bad happening to human.

But in divinely world food is not available , they depend on human only for food . although they have more sense than us , they have to take from us only .

The almighty , ultimate Gods made this connection , humans for this world will provide food to divinely persons , divinely persons will provide blessing to human. If this link is not there, both will be separated .

Hence providing food to God is main tradition in our culture. providing food to crows, street dogs etc., everything in some form it will reach the divinely Gods.

****

Home.(Veedu)

Divinely places also has time limit , after some time it will be destroyed , pleasure in divinely world also have limitation . sorrow also amiable there .

Places where there is no suffering , only pleasure and also that pleasure is ultimate , unlimited and endless is known as Veedu (Home).

" East or west home is the best " .

In this worldly life , we feel ultimate freedom once we reach our home only . were ever we go finally we have reached our home . Our final destination is Home.

Such as, beyond divinely God's worlds, there is a place called home (veedu). We will get only pleasure in that place. There is no suffering at all . That pleasure will also be infinite pleasure. The pleasure of the limitless, endless. It will be the ultimate pleasure.

The house in ruins is, there is a limit to all the worlds and there is one day destruction for the world in which we live and Gods lives .but, there is no destruction to the place of the Veedu.

Once we reach home, we have no pain at all., Only pleasure, and that too infinite pleasure, it will also be a pleasure without destruction.

Wherever we go, we get complete freedom only when we reach our home. Similarly, when we reach the world of home(veedu) our soul get complete freedom with ultimate Endless pleasure .

Wherever go in world our final destination in our mind will be come back to home. All our journey has to end in home, or else its will not a complete journey .

All of us want complete freedom without any sorrow , all we get in home only. In this world our house is not our home, its temporary home only . in temporary home itself we feel freedom means think about the real Home (veedu).

Why we came out of our real home? , and roaming in this world , and how to get back to our home? all explained by Saiva theorist . soul which is eligible to go back to home only get attracted , and have desire to reach home .

****

Three Real Objects

The Saiva siddhantas studied deeply in their pursuit of God and formulated what they had discovered into philosophies.

Whatever we seeing in this world will destroy one day , from small object to very big monument ever thing will destroy or disappear one day . nothing is permeant in this world.

So, Saiva Siddhanties started reaching to find out stable things which exist for ever.

The three real things they discovered, i.e., three indestructible things, all other things will one day perish, but only these three things are ever-present, and it will never perish.

They are

1. Pathi i.e., The Lord

2.Pasu i.e., Soul

3.Pasam, i.e., bondage, Waste

Pathi means God, leader or head . it is a living being, it is the only one in number , by nature its devoid of likes and dislikes, don't love or hate anyone. it has all wisdom, it has all power, and thus there are many attributes of God.

Pathi (God) is like a street light , if you go near the street light, you can make use of the light , if you go away from the light, you cannot use it . street light doesn't have any love or hate on any one . it will stand still. if 100 persons come near also it won't be happy or sad. Like that god also , he won't feel happy or sad for you , he won't love or hate anybody .

The Pasu means a soul, all the souls including Human, animals , plants , stones and sand. Sand and stones also a living being which possess negligible living being characters.

Like Pathi all souls are also a living being , there are many souls which are innumerable, whose knowledge is limited intelligence. And the souls have likes and dislikes.

Pasam / soul : Due to ego , these souls get away from the Pathi/God . And mingled with ego Pasam (bondage) , in Tamil direct meaning Pasu means cow , Pasam means rope . Pasu was tied by rope , which not allowing pasu to move towards God.

God is living being , once all other souls also a part of God . all are in a mingled condition , there was no differences between soul and God. It's like one object .

God has ultimate knowledge , soul due to ego , with its small knowledge came out of God and started doing bad things . Bad things are known as Pasam or waste .

Why Souls doing bad things ? Soul nature itself doing bad things only.

Soul , It seeks to do evil., Some people do bad things some people don't do that bad things , One of the two reasons for not doing such bad things is that there is no occasion to do that thing., The another one is due to fear, We are afraid that if we do this thing, we will get caught up in something or that something bad will happen to us., this are two reasons that some people do not do bad things.

Example: First time when a person taking alcohol drinks , he feels fear , what will happen , it will spoil mind, cannot walk properly , talking non sense , if some seen , they feel bad. But once started taking slowly that fear will go away , for whatever things he got fear will happen , but he won't have fear after started doing it .

Opportunities also very important , whenever opportunities come with safe environment without any fear everyone will like to do the mistakes.

So, there is no one in this world, who is good or bad, everyone wants to do bad things when the situation arises, and it is because of circumstances, that bad people are created. Once opportunities come, and no fear, everyone will do bad things only .

Since souls want to do bad things., When the circumstances set in, souls tend to do bad things. If no harm has happened after doing such things, the soul wants to do keep doing bad things.

Soul has little knowledge only, due to ego with small knowledge get into darkness while doing bad things. Keep on doing bad things darkness will keep on growing .

****

Most degraded state of the soul

Soul started doing bad things , Darkness will start surrounding the soul. and when it keeps on doing bad things continuously, the darkness will increase for the soul, at some point it will be completely darkened, and in the dark the soul will come to a stone-like state , of no knowledge of where to go.

In complete dark condition , soul cannot move , initially it will try to move . due to full darkness and no source of little light , soul stopped its movement .

Since the soul is the object of life, it must have 1.desire 2.movement 3. Knowledge. These three are living being qualities.

Because of the little intelligence of the soul, ego developed , and trapped in the darkness . reaching a stone-like state and remaining motionless. This is the degraded state of the soul, which is also called the state of the stone.

Movement and knowledge both are living being qualities became null in darkness. Desire quality started working in full form.

The soul thus trapped in the darkness will have two thoughts, one is the hatred of being trapped in the darkness by making so much of mistakes, and the other is the desire to come out of it. Both these likes and dislikes appear to the soul , its pray to God that it should be liberated.

But God is free from likes and dislikes, God has all capability to fulfil the request of these souls in a fraction of second, because He is omnipotent, and it is very simple for Him to free these souls from that darkness.

God won't do , because he doesn't have like and dislike on anyone. Soul done mistake and get into darkness , why God has to help them . God without any movement he will stand still in his position of no love no hate on anyone/ anything. Although soul is praying towards God to help them , God almighty simple watch the soul in darkness .

Souls suffering due to their ego and mistake .if God remove the soul from the darkness means Gods is favoring the souls due to Love one them which means God nature of no love no hate character will became meaningless. So, God won't worry about the souls in dark .

****

Shivam – Shakthi

Two from of one God , Shivam & Shakthi.

Sivam means matter or mass. Shakthi means Energy . Any matter if we subdivide into a very tiny particle i.e., up to sub atomic level we found energy in that .

In fact, due to that energy present only matter from . if we remove the energy from the atom , atom will vanish .

Mass and Energy are the two from of any matter. Without mass no energy , without of mass no energy .

Gross & Subtle, Life & Death, Ying & Yang, Positive & Negative, Masculine & Feminine

Every physical aspect in this cosmos is a beautiful balance of Shiva and Shakthi. This also represents the dual nature of physical existence which dissolves away when an individual is enlightened and moves into a state of unity and then nothingness.

Shiva is the consciousness which pervades the material nature. Energy is called the Shakti. Creation is brought forwards by the combination of Shiva and Shakti. That fact is represented in the Lingam.

Shiva Shakti is the eternal couple ; forever in undivided union and abiding together as Universal consciousness. Shiva is the Transcendent Self ; the stillness from which all creations are born , made manifest through the power of Shakti.

Shiva and Shakti are indistinguishable. They are one. They are the universe. Shiva is masculine. Shakti is feminine.

In the Tantric cosmology, the whole universe is perceived as being created, penetrated and sustained by two fundamental forces, which are permanently in a perfect, indestructible union. These forces or universal aspects are called Shiva and Shakti.

The tradition has associated to these principles a form, respectively that of a masculine deity and that of a feminine one. Accordingly, Lord Shiva represents the constitutive elements of the universe, while Shakti is the dynamic potency, which makes these elements come to life and act.

From a metaphysical point of view, the divine couple Shiva-Shakti corresponds to two essential aspects of the One: the masculine principle, which represents the abiding aspect of God, and the feminine principle, which represents Its Energy, the Force which acts in the manifested world and life itself.

Shakti here stands for the immanent aspect of the Divine, that is the act of active participation in the act of creation. This Tantric view of the Feminine in creation contributed to the orientation of the human being towards the active principles of the universe, rather than towards those of pure transcendence.

Therefore, Shiva defines the traits specific to pure transcendence and is normally associated, from this point of view, to a manifestation of Shakti who is somewhat stronger (such as Kali and Durga), personification of Her own untamed and limitless manifestation.

Owing to the fact that in a way, Shakti is more accessible to the human understanding (because these regards aspects of life that are closely related to the human condition inside the creation), the cult of the Goddess (DEVI) has spread more forcibly.

****

Merciful Punishment

Degraded Souls Prayer reached God .

Goodness Shakthi Feminine form of God Shiva feels pity on them , feels sympathy on Souls for their unhappiness or difficult situation. And want to help them to come out the Degraded state .

Women will have more mercy compare to Men, Mother will have more mercy compare to father , Shakthi part of Lord shiva started showing mercy towards the souls for freedom .

Proper Punishment:

The souls in such a state of misery must suffer the reward of punishment for the wrongs they have committed.

Due to mistake souls are suffering in dark, without proper punishment if the souls are released, soul won't realize the mistake they have done.

if someone done some crime , and caught by police . he will request " Please leave me , I won't respect the mistake" if he left free immediately . he won't realize the mistake after release. He will repeat the mistake .

Without proper punishment is a person was release from the mistake, he won't feel guilt for the mistake. Until release guilt will be there but after release without punishment guilt will vanish and he will respect the mistake . But after experience of punishment, he released means he won't repeat the mistake again.

Here God is not giving any punishment to degraded souls, but creating an environment for the souls to self-realized their mistake and to come out of the darkness on their own.

Example: Someone fell down in a well , God has all power to lift him out of the well in moment , but he won't do, and also, he won't throw rope or ladder to help. In spite of that He will show the rope or ladder, the way to climb up from the well.

Punishment is for to understand the mistake completely .

And the souls must realize the mistakes they have committed on their own and attain the pleasures and sorrows of the same, and then those souls will come out of the sinful state. Experience of pleasure or pain; enjoying or suffering the effects of actions in former births.

Thus, it is said that God makes way for these souls to have experiences of pleasure and suffering, and that too God does not do, which we will come to know only when we study the philosophies in depth.

The Lord will be in a state of motionlessness without doing anything, and all this will happen by His power.

Example If there is no teacher in a class room , the students will be shouting and playing, once the teacher enters the class room , the teacher no need to say anything and all the students will be in silent.

Similarly, when God is in a state of motionlessness, philosophies arise because of His truth Shakthi. For the reason of the mistakes they have committed, the souls should experience pleasures and sorrows, enjoy it to the fullest, and be completely free from it, for which philosophies are created by the power of God.

****

Saiva siddhanta philosophy

Saiva siddhanta philosophy

God will first prepare himself because he is another state of motionlessness, from where he descends to help the soul, and the state in which the Lord prepares himself is called Siva Tattva, for example, if he wants to teach in a class, the teacher must first prepare him. He would read the lesson once in previous day and then conduct the lesson on next day in the class.

Similarly, the state in which God prepares himself is called Siva Tattva .

God is merciful and that god, who is inactive with compassion for the living beings, gradually descends.

God prepare himself in a place called Shuddha Mayai / Pure illusion .

Five Stages of Philosophy of God started to being in pure illusion.

1. **Nada Tattva:** The Lord of pure knowledge is in a state of complete remembrance, which is the form of Paramasivan, the sign of which is a line.
2. **Vindu Philosophy or Shakti Philosophy:** It is the state in which the sati, the cause of longing, begins to work, the state of the

Lord's Thiruvarutshakti, which begins to form other philosophies in conjunction with Shiva. Its shape is a circle.

3. **Sadasiva Philosophy:** By the combination of Siva and Shakti, action and knowledge are in balance. The emergence of other philosophies will be stimulated. Its shape is a combination of a circle and a line, which is the Linga form.
4. **Ishvara Philosophy:** Maheshura, the power of concealment. The process of concealing the dormant souls begins, through which the knowledge of God operates indirectly.
5. **Shuddha Vidthia:** It is in this philosophy that three Gods appear, Brahma, Vishnu and Shiva, who perform the occupations of creating, preserving and destroying . It is only now that the kriya power of action to act as a slave to divine knowledge will begin to operate in the background.

The above-mentioned five philosophies, i.e., 1.Natham 2.Shathi 3.Sadakyam 4.Isuru 5.suddha vidthai These five things take place in pure illusion, so these five are called shuddha philosophy.

Vidya tattva- Vidya philosophy –knowledge philosophy .

The Lord, who has mercy on the living beings, has descended as philosophies, and the souls who are now in a stone-like state should be made to prepare in to perform action , preparing action plan for the soul is called Vidya philosophy or knowledge plan . In seven stages action plan is made as follows .

1. **Philosophy of Time:**

In this philosophy time is created. time is the determination for souls to function. God Yama arise in this philosophy . , he will take care of the time. He will provide proper time to each soul based on action plan of the souls .

2. **Justices Philosophy** : Selection of action

This Justices philosophy lists the mistakes committed by souls , select the matured mistakes and determines which pleasures and sorrows and experiences should provide for the soul to come out of those mistakes. The mistake they have made must be a mature and eligible to be cure.

Example: Seeds of plants like mango tree, coconut tree, mustard fenugreek, each seed will germinate at different time, mustard fenugreek etc. will germinate in the same day, it will take a few weeks for the mango seed to germinate. It takes a few months for the coconut tree to germinate .

Similarly, mistakes made by the souls take different periods to mature.

And also depends on soul maturity level he will select the mistake , God will not give all punishment in a single birth , depends on soul level he will select the action plan .

3. **Woke up Philosophy .**

As soon as the list of actions and the time for them are prepared, the Lord will dissolve the soul in the state of stone a little, and the soul which was now immobile will have some movement.

It is similar to Woking up a person in a deep sleep. Before opening the eyes or before coming out of sleeping mode , little movement will come .

God woke up be soul which in Stone like condition , since soul is living being slowly living being characters will come . slowly energy will come to the soul .

There are three powers for living things, one is desire, which is called Sariya Shakthi energy, the second action movement energy is called kriya Shakthi, and the third is knowledge which is called Gnana Shakthi.

As soon as the stone-like soul begins to do so, its three energies begin to form one by one. First the power of knowledge is formed, then the kriya power that begins the action.

4. **Gimmick Philosophy (Vithtai Thathuvam)** The formation of the power of knowledge and power of movement or performance is called the philosophy of Gimmicks.

5 . **Desire Philosophy: Aragam Philosophy**

As soon as the power of knowledge and power of action are formed, soul want to do some action . Soul got desire to perform action to come out of the sinful stage. This desire arises stage is called Desire philosophy.

6. Purusa: Shirt Philosophy :

Once the above mentioned five philosophies are established, i.e., time, action plan , woke up , Gimmicks and Desire , soul will get a shape . All the above philosophies are like a shirt to soul . Astral form like a hollow man , soul will be invisible only but visible with presences of this shirt .this shirt like formation is known as Anjugajam , once the soul got the kanjukas/**anjugajam** (shirt) the soul will have a form, which will be in the subtle form. The same is called as purusa Or purudan . this all development is called as Pursa philosophy or Shirt Philosophy .

7. Prakriti Maya: World Illusion .

PRAKRITI MAYA is THE WOMB OF CREATION

Formation of our earth is happening in prakriti maya, maya means illusion .

Above said 7 philosophies namely , 1.Kalam(Time), 2. Needhi (Justices) , 3. Kalai (woke up) 4. Vithtai (Gimmicks) 5.Aragam(desire to act) 6.Purudan(Astral Form) 7. Prakriti Mayai(Womb of Creation)

These are the seven philosophies and the Vidhya philosophies are instruments of the activity of the souls. Are form in the asuddha Maya . Prakriti maya also created from asuddha maya.

The five philosophies of Shiva arose out of the pure illusion, the Vidya tattvas arose out of the impurity illusion.

Formation earth will happen in 24 stages(philosophies) all happen in Prakriti Maya(World Illusion) so this maya/illusion is called as Womb of Creation.

Pure illusion and impure illusion are not taken as philosophies, but this Prakriti Maya illusion is considered as philosophy. Because this illusion is formed from the asuddha maya(impure illusion) and one among 7 philosophies in Vidya tattva- Vidya philosophy –knowledge philosophy .

In this illusion only soul is going to perform activities . so, this illusion to suite living being to be active.

Totality of the mind

As soon as the soul acquires an astral form called purusa, the Antahkarana started developing , Antahkarana refers to the totality of the mind; a four-tiered instrument of awareness.

The Antahkarana functions in four different ways. Accordingly, it gets four different names concerning the kind of part it does.

Manam: Manam refers to the mind. Therefore, it expresses itself as indecisive and agitated.

Buddhi: Likewise, Buddhi refers to the intellect. Thus, decisiveness and rational thinking is what depicts buddhi.

siddha: When working as a part that aids memory, indicates to the Citta state of mind.

Agankaram: Lastly, when a sense of individuality or ego works out (I-thought) works out, it goes by the name agankaram.

siddha is also called "prakriti". Therefore, all these twenty-four theories of mind, which are based on the mind, are called "prakriti maya theories". It is the conclusion of Saiva philosophy that when the soul and the mind (one of the Vidhya philosophies) merge with Prakriti, it begins to function in the physical world together with other philosophies. Antahkarana is a collective term for the 4 tattvas-Prakrti, buddhi, ahamkaram and manam.

1.Siddha

2.Buddhi

3. Ahamkaram

4. Manam

Knowledge tools Gnanendriyas (sense organs).

After getting mind tools , mind is ready to work for the astral soul . mind want some information , without any input information, mind cannot function .

Some inputs tools are required for the mind to get information. Otherwise, mind will be idle .

So, input devices are created they are called as Knowledge tools Gnanendriyas.

Five sense organs are created from the Mannam

The five sense organs are the

- nose, i.e., the medium to experience smell
- tongue, i.e., the medium to experience taste
- eye, i.e., the medium to experience sight
- skin, i.e., the medium to experience touch
- ear, i.e., the medium to experience sound

They are in from of following philosophy

1. Eyes

2.Ears

3.Nose

4.Tounge

5.Skin

All these things are Gnanendriam. Soul getting knowledge of outside because of this tool . mind receive knowledge from these 5 tools only.

Action Tools, Karmenthiriyam Motor Organs.

Once mind tools started receiving information's from sensor organ , sous are ready to ready action . for action 5 tools are created from following philosophy.

1.the voice,

2.the legs,

3.the arm,

4.the excretory organs (anus and urethra),and

5.the genitalia

The instruments of action arise from the quality of Rajasam gunam.

1. Voice - vakku philosophy , whatever words we pronouncing have to power of action . All the words uttered refer to an action.

2. Legs - pada philosophy Pada means feet, the foot is very essential for the movement of soul from place to place, which is called legs philosophy.

3.Arms – Pani Philosophy, Pani means hand, hands are very essential for us to pick up an object and use that object, so the philosophy of arms develops.

4. Excretory organs - The soul needs energy to function, the absorption of energy from other substances and the excretion of unwanted substances is called excretory , Bayu means digestive system , e.g., the addition of nutrients from the food to our body and then the excretion of waste products from that food. so, the philosophy of Excretory organs develops.

5. Genitalia – Reproductively Organs Upastha: Upastha means the philosophy of the formation of the genitals and the natural genital organs of the living beings.

These five instruments are the tools of action used for the operation of living beings.

Sensational/Attraction Elements : Dhanmatrai

For the souls, Function of mind created , organ for knowledge input to minds created , tools to perform action created . although all above created for doing performance some desire is required.

For example, you have one TV, power connection given , network connection give, remote given . although you got all the above, should have desire to watch some program then only you will switch on the TV . otherwise, TV will be in off condition only .

So next attracting elements created. so, the souls will get attracted towards that and start to do some actions.

From the mode of mind Tamasa there appears five for delusion, which are called dhanmatra, tanma means experiences of pleasure and suffering, or actions, and the five philosophies arise to obtain these actions or experiences of pleasure and suffering.

1. Sound

2. Pickle (touch)

3. Light

4. Taste

5. Smell

All the five types are attraction elements which give desire to soul.

Elements of earth : Place of action .

Now for the souls, Function of mind created, senor for knowledge input created, tools to perform action created .attracting elements to attracting soul to perform action also created.

Now place to perform action is to be created, earth (Bootham-5 elements of earth) is created from the sensational attraction elements .

Following philosophy created.

1. The sky- : The first thing that arises out of its earth element is Sky or Space , from the sound. For thing to stand or to be present some space is required. Hence space is created. Sky has only one sense that is sound senses only .

2. Air: From the sense of touch , air is originated . Air has two senses i.e., Sound and touch senses. Sky merged with touch sense and deformed in to air .

3. Fire: Fire arises from light, which has three characteristics, sound, touch and light. Air is mingled with light energy and deformed to fire.

4. Water: It arises from the taste, which will have characteristics i.e. sound, smell, light, and taste. Fire is deformed to water with sense of taste. Without water we cannot feel the taste. Water is created from fire with sense of taste .

5. Land: Land is the soil which arises from its or smell, which has five attributes. That is, sound, smell, light, taste and smell.

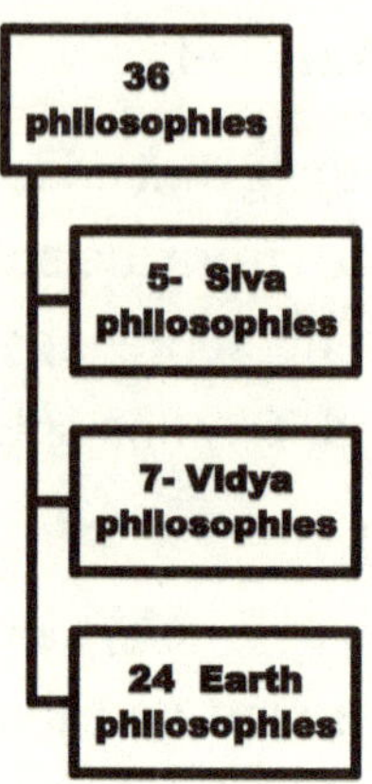

These are the 36 philosophies created by souls to satisfy their karma.

Dhanu Karana Bhavana bhogam, Dhanu means body, Karana means tools, Bhavana means place, bhogam means happiness and suffering experiences.

So, a soul in the medium of action, the instruments for which those factors create a habitat for it, and the five elements. The 36 philosophies are created by souls in order to get punishment or rid of the wrongs they have committed.

In this way, God sets up a platform for the living beings to operate , and that is the 36 philosophies.

God Philosophy : God prepared himself in Suddha maya (Pure Illusion) in 5 stages

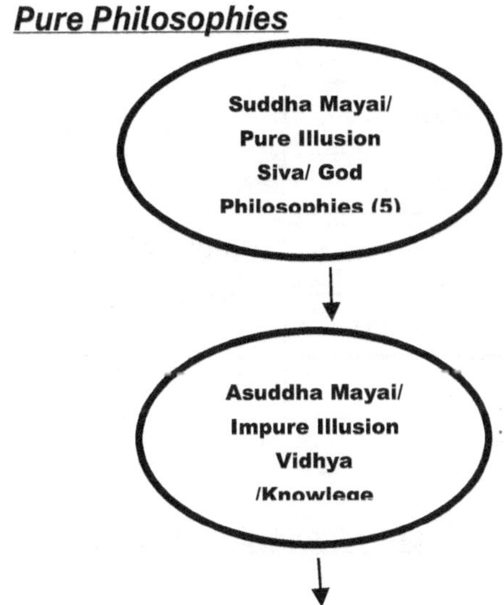

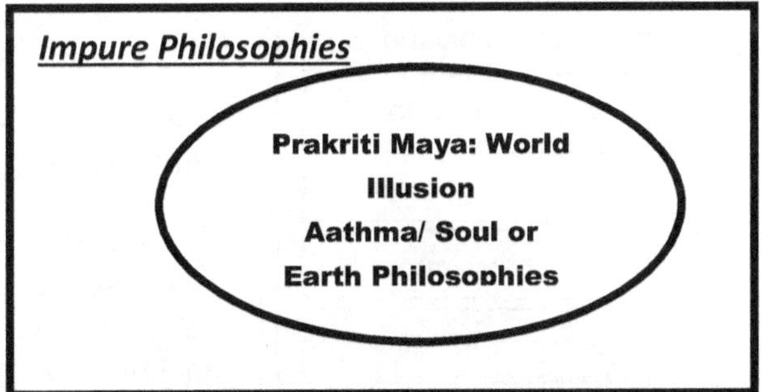

Pure Philosophies

God Philosophies and Knowledge philosophies are known as Pure Philosophy

Siva Thatuvam God Philosophy

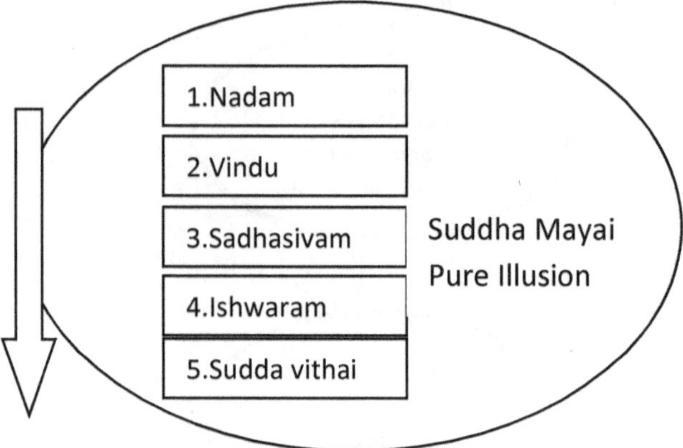

Vidhya Thatuvam –Knowledge Philosophy

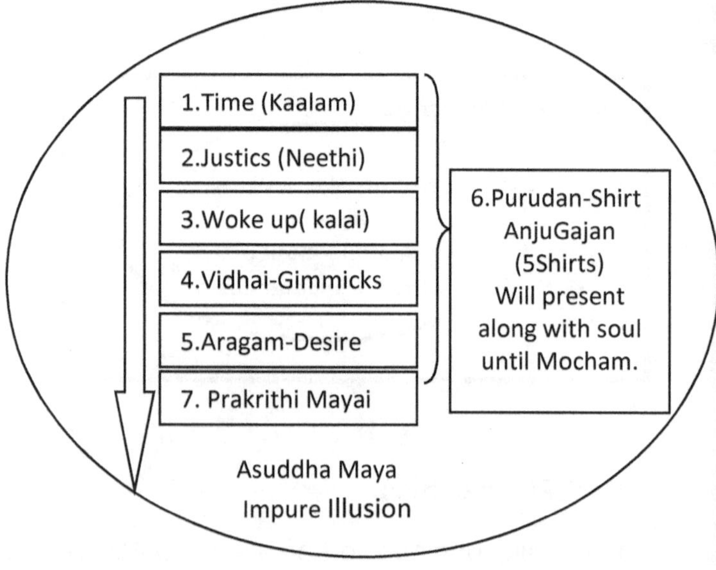

Impure Philosophies- Earth Illusion .

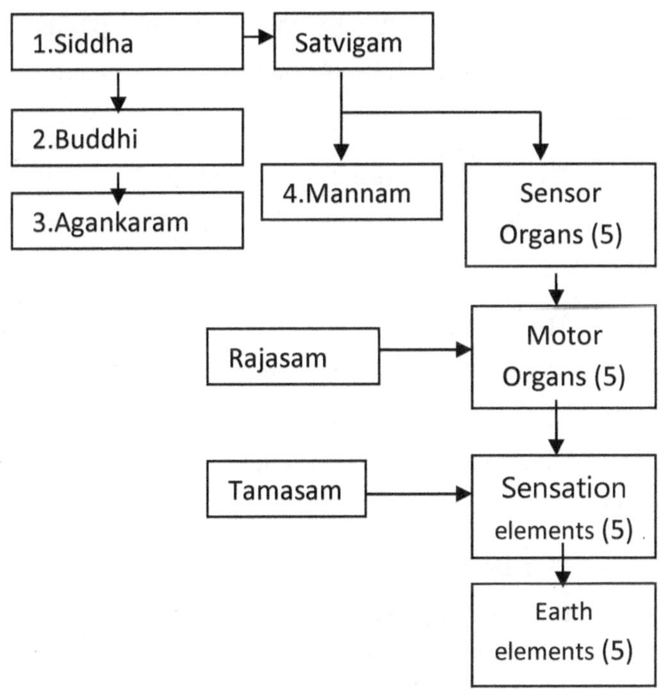

Mind tools- Antahkaranam 4

Sensor organ – Gnanendriyam -5

Motor Organ- Karmendriyam-5

Sensations – Thanmatirai - 5

Earth Elements –Pancha bhutam 5

Total 24 Philosophy from Womb of Earth

(earth illusion) Prakrithi maya.

Vidhya Philosophy : He prepared action plan, and time target time , for the soul to perform , and give knowledge to soul to perform. Womb of earth creation is created . It happens in impure illusion in 7 stages.

Mind , Body , organs , sensational elements, earth elements all are created in 24 stages. In earth Illusion.

The purpose of our current existence on this earth is to live out our vinai. (vinai in Tamil is better known as Karma. the effects of our past actions). To live out our vinai, we are blessed with a physical body.

Our body is called Thanu. The effects of our past actions in the previous birth determines the kind of body we have taken in this life. Each of us have been given instruments such as nose, ear, eyes etc. also called as Karunam, and we have been allotted a place to live out our vinai. That is, we are born in a particular country for a specific reason. That place is called Bhuvanam.

The physical objects that we are blessed with in order to live out our experiences, are called Bogam. Once our vinai is over, we will leave our Thanu, Karana, Bhuvana, Bogam and move on.

****

The Five Works of God

The Lord performs five occupations to direct lives, namely, creation, preservation, destruction, concealment and grace.

Creation: The world is flesh; Without knowledge. Life, siddha, is intelligent. The good and the bad that happens in the world are not for the object without knowledge except for the object of knowledge. Therefore, the occupation of "creation" is to unite the two by organizing the world without knowledge in such a way that it can be supplemented by the intelligent creature.

"The type of companion of life" is the desire they desire. Although these options are innumerable, they are included in the three "this world, the hereafter, and the house". Some living beings are immersed in this world; Some will be interested in the hereafter; some will be his own in the house. All this cannot be achieved without the body of living beings. Therefore, 'creation' is the arrangement of the body, etc., to life according to the will of the living beings.

We know very well that the world is a matter of things and that "maya" is the cause of it. It can be clear that "creation" is the creation of the world and adding it to the living beings from illusion .

The world, which is derived from the illusory material object, is of four kinds, namely, "Dhanu, Karanam, Bhuvana and Bhoga". Tanu is sick; Karanam is the nucleus of the mind, etc. (those karanas); Bhuvanam is a place to browse; Bhoga is the object of consumption. We know that the religious people are obsessed with the fact that God created life not in one category, but because of the actions of them, that he created many kinds of differences. This reaction is the option mentioned above. It is the result of creation to find a way to get rid of the willingness created.

Protecting: "Kaaththal" is the process of stopping and using the Dhanu Karana Bhavana bhogas given by the Lord from being destroyed. Therefore, the living beings should stand on the path of fulfilling their will and fulfill it in such a way. It is clear that 'preservation' is auxiliary process. The purpose of preservation is to stand in the way of deactivation and get the reaction removed.

Destruction: As stated in this way, "destruction" is the separation of Dhanu Karana Bhavana bhogas so that they can be born and then get rid of the state of death and be inactive in the worlds of this world and the hereafter. Therefore, the result of destruction is the removal of fatigue in births and deaths. In this way, we can know that the three occupations of God are useful for life.

The five occupations: Apart from the three occupations mentioned above, saiva siddhanta also speaks of two other occupations, namely, "concealment " and "grace". Hides the knowledge of living beings? It stimulates its hidden energy and is illusory. 'Concealment' is the creation of worldly happiness by means of kanmas and making God direct himself to the living beings and make himself look towards the world. Due to this action, the energy of the ego will decrease over time and run away. This is the use of concealment.

Arrogance . As soon as the energy has run away, the desire to seek God for living beings occurs, and when the Lord shows Himself and removes the living beings from the stools and attains Himself, is called "grace". Therefore, the lord's feet are to receive bliss, which is happiness. Grace is the result of business. By these statements and the above three, the occupations of God are created, preserved, destroyed, concealed, and bestowed upon him. These five are the 'five works' performed by The Lord for the sake of living beings.

After reaching the house, the living beings do not need Dhanu Karanam, etc.; However, dhanukarana, etc., are 'essential' in order to go on the path of attaining the attainment of that house. Therefore, the Lord gives Dhanu Karanam etc. to those who seek the wealth of the house in order to achieve it.

You have to know that you are giving and keep it in mind.

****

God in Different levels

Image - Statue, Face | Hand | Worship by giving the form of human being.

Impersonal - Linga , no human form, some symbolic form which is not look like a human .

Aruvam - formless form of worship. the state of being attached to the mind

Swaroopam – the state in which our mind cannot understand it . high level of God form.

These four are God form in Tamil worship .

Thus, the worship of God can be divided into four parts. That's because, in order to understand something, we need to know from its basic things,

if we are praying to God, we need to know God according to our knowledge, and gradually we can learn about God.

Example: When we are studying mathematics, we must first learn the order of numbers, the order of numbers is the value of each number, which is the first mathematics to learn. Only if you know the numbers in this way can you move on to the next level in mathematics.

In the second stage, have to learn basic things like addition, subtraction, multiplication division in those numbers. We deal with the numbers we have learned in the first stage in various ways in the second stage, which is the second stage of mathematics. Thus, we have to master the addition of numbers, subtraction, multiplication, division, etc., for which we have to do a number of exercises.

It is only , after we have passed the second stage , we will be able to come to know the higher level of mathematics, such as differential, integration, etc.

Thus, for the student practicing mathematics at a higher level, mathematical knowledge, such as the order of numbers and the second addition subtraction etc. should be known , which is the initial levels, the most basic knowledge, but they are the basic thing that makes them deal with mathematics, for high level students' basic levels are not mathematics for them.

Someone studying high level , with knowledge of first stage i.e., he does not know the order of numbers. If he goes directly to the second stage, he will not be able to know the mathematics of addition, etc., so he must first master the first stage and go to the second stage , only after practicing it and fully knowing the order of the numbers he will be able to understand second stage.

One who knows the order of numbers does not necessarily have to keep on practicing in the first stage itself, he must go to the second level. In the first stage, you know the numbers and stand in the first position and telling this math's means no use of it . If he does like this , his knowledge will not develop.

To him in the second position, the order of numbers does not appear to be a mathematics, but to the first, the order of numbers appears to be mathematics, and the order of numbers is the order of numbers for them. The order of numbers is a fundamental thing.

Thus, as we learn mathematics, we gradually pass through these stages and move to a higher level.

This is not only for mathematics, but in all things, we have to learn from the basics to the other and reach its highest level.

We have to learn according to our knowledge , at the level at which it is, if we are learning in a state below our level of knowledge, our knowledge will not grow, we will not be able to move towards a higher level, we will not understand anything if we start learning directly at the higher level, so it is very important to learn gradually.

Similarly, in order to know God , we have to move step by step in order to become associated with that God. The real purpose of life is to understand God according to our level of knowledge and to merge with God as one.

In our way of worship, we first give our form human being form to know God, that is, the stories, mythologies, etc. about God that we read, which depict God as human beings, all basically help us to understand God easily.

Example: If you speak in Tamil to a person who knows Tamil, he will understand, just as we human beings will get to know God in a simple way by portraying God as a human being. It is worshiping the God on the outside of our mind, to worshiping God in Statues and the temples worship etc.

The next constant image is that there will be an image but it will not be in the human form. It is the worship of the impersonal form to worship the Lord by giving him a different form and not giving him a human form. Those who worship in this state will know that God is not in a human form.

They will be in a position to worship the Lord both on the outside and within our mind.

Without going to the temple imagining the God in Temple and praying .

Aruvam: For those who worship Aruvam, the Lord does not need any form and they can worship the Lord without any form, they are capable of worshipping the Lord with in mind . According to them, idols and temples are not all forms of worship, they will not go to any temple, but their superior devotee to God then the above two types of worship

Swaroopam : Swaroopam is a state beyond the reach of our human intellect, and when we worship in that state, we become one with God, which is called mixing with one another. We cannot know this form of worship. This is a very high level.

Example: All the objects we see in this world are generally in three states.

Status of the ingredients refers to one of the various states in which an object can be found. Generally according to physics, objects can be in three stages. They are Solid, liquid, Gas are. An object in a solid state Volume, Shape and Form Will remain unchanged. Even if the volume remains unchanged in the liquid state, The shape takes the shape of the container containing it. In the gaseous state, objects have no fixed volume or shape. It can be spread all over the available space.

In recent times, Differences between the positions of an object For molecules explained in terms of the interactions between. Accordingly, a solid is a state in which the attraction between molecules keeps them stable.

Although the attraction between the molecules in the liquid state keeps the distance between them unchanged, do not keep them in a constant contact.

The attraction between molecules in the gaseous state has little effect on the movement of the individual molecules.

High at very high temperature ionization Between the molecules of the reaching gases Attractive Keys Pushing forces also create distinctive characteristics. Thus, this state is considered to be the fourth stage of the object.

It is Plasma is called a state. The plasma state is the state of the largest visible object in the universe.

Solid, - image level / idolatry

Fluidity,- Impersonal state / Impersonal worship

Gas- Aravam Status/ Aruvam Worship

Plasma- The state of the embodiment / worship of the embodiment.

Thus, the worship of God can be divided into four parts.

That's because in order for us to understand something we need to know it from the basic things, if we are to cling to God, we need to know God according to our knowledge, and gradually we can learn about God.

****

Different Methods of Worship.

There are two kinds of human beings, one side is based on emotion and the other is knowledge based.

Their religious beliefs also will be the same, in fact, every human being belongs to a different religion, and the religious beliefs will be different.

Between the brothers and sisters in the same house, the character and customs of one person will not be the same as that of the other.

No of religions in this world is equal to no of human in world , that every human being is a different religion. Every one belief is different from others . So, it is not possible if everyone has a religion in common method of worship .

But it can be broadly classified to two types , emotional and knowledge .

The path to God is divided into two, one is the emotional path and the other is the path of knowledge. This is because in general, the action of human beings is of two kinds, one dependent on consciousness and the other on knowledge.

Those who are conscious choose the path of devotion to reach God, and those who are intellectually inclined choose the path of philosophy.

The kitten and the monkey cub can be told as an illustration of this, the kitten will be carried in its mother's mouth, but the monkey cub will hold the mother, and wherever the mother monkey goes, the baby will take hold of the mother.

Which of these is the safest , is that mother hold the baby , which refers to the path of devotion. It is not possible if everyone follows the path of safe bhakti devotion , for the one who is able to acquire knowledge does not follow the path of devotion bhakti, he follows the path of philosophy. Although the two paths are different, in the end the destination will be the same.

Four Types of Worship.

Worship is divided into four types: charya , kriya, yoga and Gnana. If it is right, worshiping God in the Puram, worshipping God externally and internally, yoga means the worship of God within, and jnana means the union with God.

Charya: When going to the temple, it is okay to simply go without complete devotion. Saiva Siddhanta accepts it as a form of worship also. Like this only worship begin initially .

Kriya: worshipping the Lord by believing in the Lord, going to the temples to worship the Lord , in difficult time remember and worship the Lord with one's mind. Worship will also take place outside and inside the mind .

Yoga worship: They do not go to a temple where yoga worship is performed and worship the Lord only within themselves.

Gnana Worship: The worship of knowledge is when we mix with God and become God. This worship is the best form of worship of all.

Their position of worship is that the system of worship is not always the same and it keeps changing.

These will not be complete and can still be divided into 12 categories, in combination of these four types , example Charya in Kiriya , Charya in Yoga , Charya in Gnana , Kriya in Charya , kriya in yoga , kriya in Gnana, Yoga in seria , Yoga in Kiriya , Yoga in Gnana , Gnana in seria , Gnana in Kriya , Ganan in Yoga .

Further also it can be classified in three combinations , Charya in kriya & yoga , Charya in kriya&gnana. Like that there is endless types of worship in world . which will equal to no persons in world.

Basically, all worship will come in this category only Charya , Kriya , Yoga , Gnana.

Charya is basic of worship of God, once we started following Charya , slowly our worship will move towards Kriya , then to Yoga and final it will reach Gnana.

In Gnana is worship which happen along with God. Soul will be mingled with God. And no different between God soul at the stage .

****

Desire To reach home

Wherever we go, we get complete freedom only when we reach our home. Similarly, only when we reach the world of home, our soul will get complete freedom.

For those who know the path to reach that house, it is not only enough to know the path, but they should be mature enough to reach that house.

Thus, there are four things which is very supportive to the souls/human beings attaining home. They are 1.Aram means Dharma, 2.Porul means Artha 3. Inbam means love. Veedu –home Moksha -.

In this, home is a step towards reaching home. How's that? If we go up a staircase, the last step of that step can be called a step or a level/floor . In the same way, one has to go through the step of home to reach home.

The home is something that cannot be explained by our thinking, and it is very difficult for us to know it. It cannot be described in words and emotions .

For example, someone asking for an address of a house . If the addressed house is visible to our eyes, "here it is , that house only “ we can easily show .

suppose that address is too far away, we cannot show the house , we can tell the way only to reach that address, but we cannot show it directly.

Similarly, home cannot be explained by words.
But it can be explained by following Asceticism

Aram means Dharma , : Dharma is doing right things , and not doing wrong things .

If you are not doing anything , fully idle , means you are not doing wrong things also , then is it’s called as dharma , is it so ? No, not doing wrong thing also drama , but not doing right thing is against dharma , so always we have done some action that too right things.

There are three types of this Dharma. They are called discipline, litigation and punishment /penalty.

Discipline varies depending on the profession we do. For every profession, what has been said to be moral is observed regularly by those who are engaged in that profession. For example, for a soldier it is discipline to shoot an enemy, and for a student it is discipline to study.

litigation is a tool to find out the truth. It's like we're arguing in court today. Two people claim to one thing separately, one says mine, and the other also says mine, in this someone is lying , litigation is to find out saying the truth.

A penalty is a punishment given to those who have failed in discipline, after finding out through a litigation that they have deviated from the moral code, so that to make them to act morally again.

So, punishment is not only a punishment for a mistake they have committed, it is also a punishment for correct them self to avoid mistake again .

Thus, the Litigation and the penalty are used to keep us in discipline , and discipline is the best thing to life. The litigation and penalty are only to be used to follow discipline. So, they are not so important Dharma then discipline .

Similarly, we can naturally, by our senses, know the litigation and the penalty. Naturally, we know that if we make a mistake, we will be punished.

We know that many days a thief will one day be caught, and we know that if we commit a mistake, we will be caught in a case and will be punished for this .

Therefore, the discipline of excellence is called Dharma.

Porul means Artha : Wealth is not only related to earning Money , its related to learning about worldly life , its most important for one to have good attitude and good behavior , this world is a good teacher to teach the right things to us . which will be useful for us to attain our Home (Veedu Peru) .

Pleasure : what is Real pleasure , real and ultimate pleasure is available in veedu , when we are mingling with God in veedu , at that stage we will enjoy endless , limitless and ultimate pleasure .

Who want pleasure , first we should know what is pleasure , then only our soul will have desire to get real pleasure .

Without knowing what is pleasure , who will like to have the pleasure .

For example : a person , who never taken non vegetarian food , he never tasted a Mutton biryani, chicken biryani . another person taken non veg foods .

If someone says to both of them, one hotel in there in Chennai , where very good non veg food are available , different kind of sea foods are available, some food only there only available . very delicious foods .

In this the person who has experiences in taking non veg food only get desire to take that food in that particular hotel. Another person who never taken non veg food least bother about the hotel.

A person who tasted little pleasure only have desire to get more and more pleasure .

In Tamil culture says two type of pleasure, setruinbam & perinbam(small pleasure & big pleasure) . one is limited pleasure another one unlimited pleasure .

Unlimited pleasure is whatever activates you doing for God , thinking, singing, dancing , talking &prayers etc. all known as unlimited pleasure things . Limited pleasure is all other things whichever is not related to God.

How we are getting and feeling pleasure, all through our sense organs only , i.e., Eyes, Nose, ears, tongue & Skin.

A jasmine flower it will give pleasure to eyes and nose. Listening songs it will give pleasure to ears , watch a movie will give pleasure to eyes, ears , eating good food will pleasure to tongue and nose . Is there anything which gives pleasure to all the five organs at a time.

Yes, pleasure of love between a male and female , this the only thing in this world which gives you pleasure to all your sense organ at a time . girl is getting pleasure from boy ; boy is getting pleasure from a girl . that too with proper marriage in an ethical way .

In an unethical way someone wants to enjoy this pleasure it will end up in misery only. It will spoil your values in tall terms .

Pleasure which is giving happiness to all the five sense also called as small pleasure . then we have to think how big will be pleasure in Veedu.

For getting desire to reach home , desire to reach ultimate pleasure is important , hence pleasure play an important role in souls to reach home.

****

Thirukkural - The Way to Reach Home

Thirukkural is very useful for us to reach home, by teaching us Aram, Porul and Inbam . it's a guide for us to reaching Home . step by step thiruvallur explain the path to reach veedu .

Praise the Lord is the introduction of thriukkural , we see ways to reach Veedu in first 10 Thirukkural.

Thirukkural: 01

A is the first of the alphabet;
God is the primary force of the world.

Explanation

The sound A is the first of all letters, all the letters a is the metamorphosis of the sound A, and the letter A is naturally derived, and all the other letters appear to be in the letter A.

Similarly, this world is the metamorphosis of the Original Lord., The objects and living beings found in this world deformation of God. Therefore, the Adi Bhagavan is the first of the world.

Just as all letters arose on the basis of the letter A, so all things and all living beings arose in this world on the basis of God.

Just as the sound “A” arose naturally and all the other letters arose in relation to it, so the leadership of the Adi Bhagavan arose naturally, and everything else arose in relation to the Original Lord.

Thirukkural: 02

What is the use of all your learning,
if you can't surrender yourself at the feet of God.

Explanation

From this human state, we move from bottom to top to reach God state, God who is at the top. When we reach God, the first thing we see is the feet of God. He called it a good foot.

If we study, our ignorance will be removed , if our ignorance is removed, we will develop knowledge , and we should use that knowledge to do good to others, which is called grace.

If we have grace, we can reach God , and if we reach God, we will be immortal without birth and death.

Therefore, the purpose of the education we learn is to impart knowledge of education , and that knowledge should be used to do righteousness , and that virtue will blossom into grace . If we do so, we can reach God. So, the purpose of education is to reach God. If one reaches the Lord, one can reach a state where only happiness can be attained without birth and death.

Thirukkural: 03

Those who surrender themselves at feet of the one,

who resides in the flower-like hearts of all, will live long and well..

Explanation

No matter by what name we call God, in whatever form we think of Him, that God, in the form we thought, will come and dwell in our hearts.

Because God is one, he has no name, no form .

For example, whether you say Perumal, Murugan, Jesus or Allah, everything is one. No matter what name you worship, He will bless you.

If we worship the feet of the Lord who sits in our hearts, we can live a long life without birth and death.

There are three types of actions: thinking with the mind, speaking with the word, and doing it as an action. Worship is of three types, mental worship, word worship and action worship.

Here is telling benefits of mind worship.

Thirukkural 04

Those who surrender at the feet of the one,
who doesn't have wants or hates, will never have any hassles anywhere.

Explanation

God has no likes and dislikes; God is free from likes and dislikes for any object . Thus, the absence of likes and dislikes is the state of the house , which is natural to God and we will get it if we try.

There are three types of congenital sufferings . One is about ourselves, i.e., we are doing harm to ourselves, for example, drinking alcohol , eating meat, smoking, etc., causing harm to ourselves by such actions, and second one is suffering from others i.e., the sufferings that may come to us by others, for example, when we are going through our vehicle properly, someone in front of us comes on the wrong path and hits us. There is nothing wrong on us but suffering is for us .through another person's fault.

The third is about the deity, i.e., God gives us some suffering, and so the sufferings that may come to us by the deity.

We will become we think , whatever we keep on thinking will convert to speech and action .

Whatever happening in life is , what we are thinking about, Ramakrishna paramahamsa, who worshipped shakti, meditated on ambal, when he wrote about him, writes that in the end his breasts began to grow like the breasts of women, and that the female form itself had begun to come to him to make him pretend to be shakti .

If we keep thinking about God, the nature of God will come to us, the nature of God is free from love and hatred, we will keep thinking about God and we will also have no likes and dislikes.

If there is no likes and dislikes, we can reach a house without birth and death, and if there is no such birth, the three kinds of suffering that come from birth will not come close to us.

If there is no likes and dislikes, no suffering will come close to us. As the Buddha says, desire is the cause of misery & suffering, God has neither desire nor hatred, and if we too got the character of no likes and no dislikes, we will not suffer from any harm.

Thirukkural: 05

Fate, which impacts those in the darkness of ignorance, will not impede those who hail the true glory of God.

Explanation

Human beings have three living being bad qualities, of which two are mainly said to be, one is lust and the other is anger, both of which are living being character, both of which are the nature of living beings. These are not coming from outside. Though the cause of lust and anger comes from outside, both of these appear within life. delusion is caused by both of these, then delusion is the misunderstanding of an object, and delusion is the understanding of right as wrong and wrong as right.

The reason for both the good and the evil that we can do is because of seduction. No one can say clearly about starting of lust and anger, which is so seduction, is of any nature, nor can anyone say how it appears, and therefore these are called darkness.

Good deeds about doing good , and evil is doing evil.

That is, these are the two reason that cause our birth to continue . Even if you do good deeds, the birth will continue and the birth will continue even if you do evil also.

If we want to reach a house without destruction, we have to reach a state where there is no birth and death . Therefore, reaction of good action and evil action should not be with us.

If we praise those who do not have the qualities of God, i.e., human beings, then all those praises are meaningless, meaningless fame.

It is said that if we praise God constantly and constantly, then lust and anger will not come to us, if neither of these things come, then there will be no seduction, seduction is darkness because of delusion, we will have no reaction of good & evil, and if there is no reaction of good and evil actions , then there will be no births because of it. If there is no birth and death, we can reach home and attain an indestructible life which gives us indestructible happiness.

Thirukkural:06

Those who follow the true moral path of the one, who has doused the desires of the five senses, will last long.

Explanation

All the desire that comes to us comes through the organs, and those organs are the five organs eyes, nose, the ear, tongue& Skin .

The desire is the same , for example, you saw the Tirupati laddu, and when you see that laddu, the color of that laddu goes through your eyes and arouses desire, the smell that comes from that laddu will go through you and arouse your desire, and when someone says 'Tirupathi laddu', the word will go through your ear and arouse desire for you . Similarly, as soon as you touch that laddu, that desire will appear through your fingers, and if you start eating that laddu, its taste will go through the tongue and arouse the desire you want. Thus, desire is the source of the five organs but desire is the same.

Thus, the desire reaches us through our five organ and

God don't have these five kinds of desire and we human beings can without this desire by effort, some monks do not have these desire , even if they do have, they have done with effort to remove all desire, but for God it is natural, by nature god don't have desire.

It is God who has given us the meaning of righteousness in this world with nature, and whoever says righteousness, God is the owner of that virtue. The true moral code speaks of the righteousness so prescribed by God.

Those who live in that moral code will live long and long as they are one and the same for all time.

So, morality belongs to God, that God is devoid of aspirations, and if we follow the moral code of God, we can live without birth and death.

Thirukkural: 07

Except for those who surrender at the feet of the one, for whom,
there is no simile, it is tough to cure the mental rues.

Explanation

If you worship, you can attain liberation , but if you don't worship, you can't change your small worries also .

When comparing a person to one another, in one case they may have similarity , but in another case we can't compare .

Example An actor is very handsome but his knowledge is a little less, it is correct if we mention his beauty that there is no one who is equal to this actor, it is not right if we say that there is no match for that actor, because even if there is no match for his beauty there will be people who are equal to him in other respects.

But as far as God is concerned, there is nothing equal to God in any matter. We cannot refer to anything as a parable to The Lord, there is no one similar to God in any aspect .

If you are not thinking about the God, you cannot remove your mind sorrows in mind.

If the sorrows in mind is certain then birth is certain , if birth is certain then death is certain, if birth is certain then lust, anger and seduction are certain, if seduction is certain, then suffering is certain, and for all but those who have attained to God, the suffering due to seduction is certain.

If we do not worship the Lord in mind always, we will not be able to attain the state of unbornness, and the birth will continue, and so will the suffering that comes from the delusion of lust and innocence will continue. If we constantly think of the feet of the Lord, we can reach home by mental worship, otherwise we will not be able to reach home.

Thirukkural: 08

Except those who surrender at the feet of God, the ocean of morality,
others will struggle to cross the ocean of desire.

Explanation

If we are to travel in righteousness, which extends like the sea, we must constantly think of the feet of God.

Just as we need a boat to sail in the sea, we have to touch the feet of God to travel in the sea of righteousness.

If we think that we can achieve wealth and happiness without walking in the way of righteousness, it will not happen. Why if

Righteousness is called the body of God, and if you walk contrary to righteousness, it is equivalent to beating the body of God. If you do so, you will not get any wealth or happiness.

If we are constantly thinking of the feet of the Lord who is the ocean of righteousness, we can cross that trust (let us live in the way of righteousness) otherwise we cannot live according to righteousness, if we do not live according to righteousness, we will not be able to reach home, if we do not reach home, birth and death will continue, in this ocean of life we will not be able to cross the shore.

Moreover, if there is no virtue, we are unable to enjoy wealth and pleasure.

Thirukkural: 09

The head that doesn't bow to God, is similar
to the organs that don't have the right senses.

Explanation

It is of no use if we don't have the action of these five-sense organ, that we have if they are not working in the principle of them .

It is of no use of sense organs, if do not have its principle, such as the invisible eye and the ear that does not hear. If the principle means that it does not have the capacity supposed to have, the eye means to see, and if it cannot see from the eye, then the eye is called the eye without principle. and there is no use in a head that does not worship the foot of the Lord who possesses eight qualities.

God qualities are

1.Becoming self-made - the one who is created by himself,

2.One who has a pure body - the body we have is an impure body, the body of God is a pure body.

3. Ultimate understanding -conscious means one who is naturally capable of perceiving everything.

4. Ultimate knowledge ; To feel the whole- to know everything and to know it fully.

5. He who naturally removes affections- None of these affections that human beings have, and are not naturally to God.

6. He who has the great grace- We know that grace means grace, and perarul means the quality of God.

7. Possession of energy in the end- it means one who has infinite energy

8. Happiness in the range - means one who has infinite happiness, which is said in Saivism.

It is difficult for us to understand these qualities so that we cannot measure by thought, and it is impossible to understand the qualities of God.

To say that there is no use in the head that does not worship feet of the Lord is of no use is an act. there is no use in a head that does not worship the Lord. The tongue is in the head is of no use of it also .

Thirukkural: 10

Those who surrender at the feet of God,
will cross the great ocean of life; others won't..

Explanation

The ocean of birth, birth is like a great sea because just as the waves come and go in the sea, so does birth and death, the waves come from the sea towards the shore and then go towards the sea , and then it goes towards the sea because it has come towards the shore because the shore is a mound. It is because of the coming of one wave that another wave is created and thus the waves continue to form continuously.

That is why the good that we do in this life is reincarnate by the result of evil, and the good that we are going to do in that rebirth will be reborn by evil and so on. Therefore, he described birth as an ocean.

The good or bad that we do in this life , it is matter of reincarnation. Then there is another birth that becomes due to reincarnation.

Those who belong to the Lord will reach a house without birth and death, and those who do not belong will be immersed in this ocean of birth and will be without shore.

Worshiping God is very important to achieve God nature of “no like” & “no dislike” with in our self , and we will get mingled with the God of all Origin and live an endless happy life.

Work ship is three type mind, speech , and action .

Whatever is there in the mind only will come in speech and action, so pray in mind is more important .

By this we can reach the GOD, and live in Home happily with endless and ultimate pleasure .

****

Yogic effort-Way to home.

Human beings are born with the same nature when they born, and those of them who do simple things are small persons , those who accomplish rare things that others cannot do are great persons , and the little ones do not do such great things.

Simple things are the desires and angers that our mind receives through our five senses organs , and the great things to do is practicing Yoga , which are rare things to do.

Eight types of yoga organs.

They are:

1. Yamas: external disciplines, like universal values
2. Niyama: internal disciplines, like personal observation
3. Asana: poses or postures
4. Pranayama: breath control
5. Pratyahara: withdrawal of the senses
6. Dharana: concentration
7. Dhyana: meditation
8. Samadhi: bliss, or union

1. Yamam -Removable qualities;

    It means refraining from doing bad things. Abstaining from evil deeds.

Social restraints and moral codes of yoga. The Yoga Sutra describes five different yamas, including ashimsa (non-violence), asteya (non-stealing), satya (truthfulness), aparigraha (non-possessiveness), and brahmacharya (celibacy or fidelity).

2.Niyam- Doing Good deeds qualities; That means doing good deeds. Observances, rules, and guidelines. The Yoga Sutra describes five different niyamas,
including saucha (cleanliness), santosha (contentm ent), tapas (self-discipline), svadhyaya (self-reflection), and ishvarapranidhana (surrender to a higher power).

3. Asanas: Asana means sitting, if we sit cross-legged in one place, we should sit without any movement in the body, the exercises done for this are called asana.

But today many yoga centers practice asanas , they teach that asana brings many benefits to our body, but asana is done for us to sit in one place without movement, all the other benefits to the body are incidental benefits, the real benefit of Asaam is to sit quietly in one place without any kind of pain and continue the yoga exercises.

Yoga postures or poses. The asanas emphasize the importance of caring for the body and developing the discipline to advance spiritual growth.

4. Pranayama: This is a breathing exercise, as we breathe out mind will change, it will change our qualities, ex: anyone in angry person breathes out faster. If we control the breath then we can attain the quality of meditation.

Use of breath. Pranayama consists of breathing techniques that can reduce stress and improve physical and mental health. In pranayama, you focus deeply on breath control through inhalation, breath retention, and exhalation patterns.

5. Pratyahara: This is mind control and controlling bad thoughts through good thoughts, if we think about a good thing, we don't have time to think about bad things so when bad things come in mind, we have to control them with good thoughts

Withdrawal. Pratyahara is disengaging your mind from external disturbances and controlling your reaction to them. During pratyahara, your five sense organs still detect external stimulation, but you don't allow them to disrupt your state of mind.

6. Dharana: Concentration. In Pratyahara that good thoughts arise without bad thoughts, thoughts appear in many ways, we control many thoughts and turn them into one thought.

The goal of dharana is to bind your consciousness to one particular object, place, or idea. Focusing your attention on one thing helps quiet your mind by closing off a path for other thoughts to seep in.

7. Dhyana: Remembrance; In dharana we transform many thoughts into one thought, in meditation thinking about that one thought for a long time becomes dhyana.

Meditation. Dhyana is similar to dharana, except during dhyana, you reach a state of being where you are so completely immersed in your meditation that it becomes a part of your consciousness.

8. Samadhi: Samadhi is a state of calmness, when our mind and ego are not moved by any of these things, and when life attains its natural state of

motionlessness, it is called Samadhi. In this state, the soul mixed with the Lord, there will be no difference between the Lord and this being. soul is in its natural state. Bliss or enlightenment. Samadhi is the highest state of consciousness one can achieve through meditation. It consists of a yoga practitioner reaching spiritual enlightenment where the self, the mind, and the object of meditation merge together into one.

These are the eight steps followed by yoga to attain Home.

The pleasure a living being takes in the world after birth is worldly pleasure. The pleasure of receiving the grace of God at the end of many births is called Bliss. This is referred to as Bhogam and Moksha.

Pleasure preceded by suffering. Suffering is followed by pleasure. May the Lord bless us with joy and bliss without suffering. Satnipadam is the environment in which the grace of the Lord can be obtained. Satnipadam means instillation of God's grace. In order to reach this state, there must be a state of considering pleasure and pain together in living beings.

It means to think that everything is the state of birth and should be experienced without any feeling of pleasure and pain.

To achieve this, one should follow the four principles of right, action, yoga and wisdom.

The first three are functions that living beings have to perform. Righteousness means giving charity to God and servants with the body. Kriya is a method of worshiping the forms and murthas of God. Yoga is penance by thinking of God.

If you observe these three events, you can get enlightenment from the sage who is the form of the Lord. Satnipadam (domestication) is achieved by attaining enlightenment.

****

Get home

Get home (Veedu Peru) , meaning Moksha, , Salvation “liberation,” is one of the major goals of our soul .

The idea behind “Get Home” is to achieve freedom from the cycle of life, death, and rebirth and the suffering that comes along with that cycle. There's no one way to achieve , so look for the spiritual path that feels right to you. No matter which path you choose, you'll need to focus on achieving self-control, letting go of your desires, and selflessly serving others.

In Saiva Siddhanta true liberation is a gift from God and the result of his direct intervention. When the Souls are immersed in maya, they learn about the unreal from the unreal. What they learn is basically theoretical knowledge or lower knowledge. It does not help them to transcend their conditioned minds and experience their true consciousness. It is only when Lord Siva bestows his grace upon them and comes to them in the form of a personal guru, the Souls overcome their illusion and realize their Siva consciousness.

Liberation

According to Saiva Siddhantha , liberation is attained through the means of charya, kriya, yoga and Gnana.

The path of charya involves serving Lord in a temple or religious place by performing such tasks as cleaning, cooking, carrying water, gathering flowers etc. This is called Bhakthi path, devotional path or the path of the servant. By this path one gains entry into veedu .

- The path of kriya involves performing devotional tasks such as worshipping the idol , singing devotional songs, reciting the mantras, narrating stories about God or doing personal service to God like a son does to his father. This is called the path of a good son. By following this path, one gains close proximity to Veedu.
- The path of yoga involves practicing yoga exercises (asanas) and meditation and contemplation (dhyana). By following this path, one gets an opportunity to live constantly in the company of God and become his spiritual companion. Hence this path is called path of friendship.
- The path of knowledge is the fourth path. It is the best and most direct path to the Veedu .

> The other three are actually considered inferior to it. On this path, Gnana or knowledge is the means. It is called truth-marga because it takes the Souls closer to Truth and makes it possible for them to experience or become aware of their true God consciousness.

After liberation, the liberated soul knows that its intrinsic nature is that of Siva but that it is not Siva or the Supreme Self. Thus, in its liberated state it continues to experience some form of duality, while enjoying Siva (Pati) consciousness as its true consciousness free from all bonds (pasas).

Bheda-Abheda

In Saiva Siddhanta, liberation of a Soul does not mean that its existence as an individual soul is lost forever. After liberation the Souls enjoy a special relationship with Siva called bheda-abheda (separation and non-separation), which essentially means the duality between the two (the Linga and the anga) linger, one being the whole and the other being the part, but the unity of experience prevail. The relationship is not of oneness but of sameness. In their liberated state the Souls experience unlimited bliss and freedom from the bonds (pasas) of Samsara. The Siva-gnana-bodham cautions the individual Souls who have become free while still living on earth to maintain inner purity and practice austerities so that, when they finally depart from here, the fruit of their previous actions do not interfere with their final liberation.

Saiva Siddhanta recognizes three types of Souls or souls based on their degree of bondage to the pasas or impurities. In the first category are the souls that are bound by all the three bonds (pasas) namely anava, karma and maya. In the second category are souls that free from two bonds namely karma and maya and are bound by anava alone. In the third category are souls that become free from maya only during pralaya or the dissolution of the entire creation.

****

The mystery of the creation of the world

We understood the origin of this world through 36 philosophies. Pasu the soul, turns away from The Lord , along with the arrogance of 'I am' and gets trapped in the Ego. Darkness engulfs the soul because of the Ego , and after the darkness has been completely engulfed, the soul is unable to move and stands motionless like a stone, which is the Most degraded state of the souls.

A soul that is completely trapped in dark , regrets the mistake it has made, and it has two thoughts, one is the regret of making such mistakes and getting caught in the dark, second one the desire to be free from this state and be with the Lord. So, these likes and dislikes appear in those souls.

God is all-powerful and wise. If he thinks, in a moment's time, he can free those souls from the degraded state. But god's nature is devoid of likes and dislikes. He does not do it directly any help to living beings. Through His power, the Merciful Lord renders a helping hand to liberate the souls from suffering and that is the birth of this world that we see.

It is not God who created living beings, and when God appeared, then soul also arose, and there was also an ego (waste) or bondage .

God , soul and bondage, this three are Immortal things, it is because of the feces of arrogance that the soul separated from God and became alone. Therefore, this Lord , soul and ego/arrogance /Bondage are eternal objects.

There is no beginning for them. These are all non-existent substances.

God is one, he is one. he created this world and he did not create newly, he formed the world to this form which was in some other form.

For example, we make a pot out of soil , we make that pot but we do not make the soil, we make the pot out of the soil. In the same way, God created the world in the form of subtleties into this vast world that we see now.

Souls will be fully aware of the mistakes they have made and will merge together with God after the arrogance has completely disappeared.

The soul has little knowledge, so that it cannot fully understand these Bondage/waste/ego, and to do so, the Lord creates Dhanu Karna Bhavana bhoga. Souls must be born into the world and experience pleasures and sorrows and attain maturity.

Example: If you are watching a comedy film, the first time you watch it will give you the joy that gives you pleasure, and if you see the same film again and again, the humor in it will not give you laughter or pleasure. We will take many births and come to the maturity to realize that the real happiness is the attainment of God, by destroying the experiences of happiness and suffering in these births.

Fatigue: This soul suffers from three types of fatigue, one is physical fatigue, the second is mental fatigue depression, and the third is life fatigue.

Fatigue is the fatigue in our bodies, which causes our body parts to break down after working too hard and require some rest to repair it.

Depression: Sometimes the sorrows we hear can make our mind tired and when we get tired, our body will also become tired, and in case of mental exhaustion, the body and mind will not function. For example, if someone close to us dies, our mind and body will become tired and our body will be without movement.

Life fatigue: Life fatigue is when many births are born and die and life becomes tired after experiencing many pleasures and sorrows. Such a life desires tired. Soul got tired by taking birth again and again, souls desire to reach God. It will try to reach a home that gives only happiness without birth and death.

This world was created so that souls in degraded state, who come out of that haughty. That Souls should be born in this world, have compassion for themselves, experience pleasures and sorrows, get rid of the arrogance of 'I' and unite with God.

The principle of Saiva Siddhanta is that every action has its own reaction, that the souls who have been born out of Ego arrogance perform many acts in this life, which are good and evil, and these two actions are responsible for the rebirth, and in order to get rid of the arrogance, the souls take these births and do not come out of it, but the souls perform the deeds here and take rebirth. These actions are called karma,

The desire in the actions we do is the reason for the formation of this karma, so if we perform actions without any desire, this karma will not come near us, and if we are not likes and dislikes, then no suffering will come near us.

Maya: This birth we have taken is derived from maya, which is not permanent, we have been born millions of births like this, we have millions of relationships, we have millions of relationships, so all the relations we have in this life are all an illusion, these are not permanent, we must remove attachments to these relations. Our relationship should be devoted to God and God and strive to reach God.

The creation of this world is to get rid of Ego & arrogance and merge with God. This is the secret of the creation of the world.

****

www.ingramcontent.com/pod-product-compliance
Lightning Source LLC
LaVergne TN
LVHW090123160826
845673LV00015B/831

* 9 7 9 8 8 9 2 3 3 6 9 9 4 *